circling smoke,
scattered bones

Joy McCall

Keibooks, Perryville, Maryland, USA

ISBN 978-0615880006

Keibooks
P O Box 516
Perryville, MD 21903
http://AtlasPoetica.org
Keibooks@gmail.com

for Andy, Kate and Wendy, with love

and

for Sanford Goldstein and M. Kei,
who believed

"Joy McCall takes five lines and turns each of her tanka into miniature life stories. They are rich in experience, wonder, grief, curiosity, loss and splendor, to name just a scattering of what Joy can make you feel. I often tell her how much I admire her courage, not just in the tragedies that have befallen her over the years, but as a writer tackling a difficult form and managing to squeeze so much truth out of every word. It takes guts to be so honest and daring, to love the world so much that despite great pain she not refuses to give up, but also celebrates the act of going on by feasting her eyes on everything around her. Her work offers it all, from shadow to blaze."

--Barry Dempster, author of *Invisible Dogs*

"Knowing Joy has brought more to my life than I ever could have imagined. Not just friendship, the love of poetry, not just shared laughter and tears, the witch hazel in her yard that is mine nor the golden currant in my yard that is hers. Joy may live her life with great physical limitations, but I know of no-one else whose mind and heart soar the way hers do, whose rich inner life is so dazzling.

"In this collection of Joy's tanka we are given many small perfect gifts. All I know to do is say thank you."

–Lynda Monahan, author of *A Slow Dance in the Flames* and *Verge*

"The tanka have arrived by email for years now. They rarely come alone; most often in long threads—and I scroll to read them, exploring every few days the images and ideas of my mother's writing-life. There are the old themes and characters that hold her attention, year after year. Then, there are the surprises: something new that's stepped to the fore, catching her fancy or knocking into the peace of her daily reflections like a balled-fist.

"For three decades, the great distance between our homes has brought us the challenge many families face. From so far apart, how might we share the stuff that makes our living worthwhile? For three decades, my mother has kindly and warmly met that challenge through her written words. Letters, postcards, notecards, and then, tanka. She's made it her life's work to draw beauty from terror, and comfort from desolation, and to share her understandings in poems. They are seeds, taking root in the minds of her readers. With this collection I celebrate that my mother has taught me not only how to see—but how to see with the soul, and from afar."

–Kate Franks

"As we have laughed at her house, an answer to the age-old question: 'where does the time go?'. . . the only plausible reply seemed that 'it simply turns to dust'. But for her it is not dust, in truth, but pages and pages of flowing words, each capturing a moment in a life of endless observation, musing and reflection. For me, so many moments to recall and recount, but underlying so many of them, a woman always reaching out to places and people from the closest centre to the farthest edges of her life. After parts inside were broken and disconnected, she pulled in the world, weaving words together with lives, collecting and connecting up the stories, emotions and hearts into a new network of hope, love and life, to repair what had been lost. Beauty and depth like a polished stone dropped into a clear, deep pool, to radiate Joy back out to her readers."

–Wendy Franks

M. Kei–thank you.
I am proud of this book because of you.
You made it shine.
–Joy McCall

tracing
the silver labyrinth
with one finger
always wondering
where the road will lead

Joy McCall

Table of Contents

Invocation

Magic.

There's a word to conjure with.

As you are about to feel for yourself, Joy McCall knows all about conjuring.

Word after delicately chosen word, she brings her spells to life. Be sure, however, that these words are but signs, grooved etchings that signify.

The medium is not stone, though, no; the medium wherein they are carved is flesh, the living Flesh of Self, the resonant Flesh of Other.

This Flesh is the flesh of the heart.

There is a veil in this world, a mystery. Everyone knows it, or senses it; those who don't, perhaps, sense it most of all.

Maybe more a skeptic than a believer, Joy McCall knows all about spirits for, you see, she, too, is one.

The beautiful verse, the tanka herein, are not about nature in the conventional, Western sense, not in the sense so often found in Eastern-inflected work.

They *are* nature.

There is a tactility here that is nature: the breath of it, the smell of it, the taste. One need not see, you see, to feel, nor touch to love.

going indoors,
I say goodnight
to the sky—
and the year's first swifts
come screaming over my head

There is much magic here—the believer knows it when she is confronted. Those who don't believe, but don't deny, these are the ones upon whose backs the world is borne.

This is Joy McCall: poet, conjurer, lover, friend, magician, wordsmith, witch of witches.

Sign, spirit, flesh . . .

Magic.

These, these are words to conjure with.

Don Wentworth, Poet & Editor, *Lilliput Review*

after the crash

nothing compares
to the old motorcycle
throbbing along
leaning into the bends
eating the miles—not even you

after the crash
left me paralysed
forever—
a fortune cookie:
'you will always be safe'

how strange
that I have no memory
of my left leg
which changed gear so many times
on the old motorbike

now and then
in the night, the rain
begins again,
waking me from a dream
of blood, dripping

passing the crash site
there is an eerie silence
like a gap in time
I wonder what I left there
something more than life and limb

my wedding ring
somewhere in the wreckage
on the road
my sense of safety
and simple faith, lost too

on the corner
where I crashed,
a new chapel
Plymouth Brethren pray
where my body broke

how is it
that I miss the old bike
more than my feet?
the sound of an engine
brings instant tears

beside the fields
of poppies and mustard
I weep
overcome by the longing
to walk and lie on the land

we write
of body parts,
detached
my leg, his hand; trying
to hold ourselves together

bone-bits and gravel
work their way to the surface
after all these years
the road still reminds me
how nearly it took my life

sorrow falls
a heavy dead weight
I want to go
where my feet can't take me
where love lies sleeping

when asked
what I miss most
these days
it's not standing or walking,
it's making love at bedtime

vitiligo
his skin like ancient maps
because of me
my blood and broken bones
eroding his soul

Muslim girl
doing shiatsu
on my scarred body—
the head covering
adding to her beauty

green silk

how lovely you look
in the green silk coat and hat
barefoot on the path
by the river; above you
the green silk of the willows

strange scent
of hawthorn blossom
as I pass by
into my heart creeps
one more friend

no lady
would wear pink and yellow
together
the wild geranium patch
sprinkled with buttercups

the red-faced goldfinch
is picking yellow petals
from dandelions
to line his nest with the soft
golden fragrance of flowers

the wagtails
carry the cat fur away
to line their nests
how cross the old cat would be
if he knew where his hair went

no cuckoo calls
over the hill where we sit
listening
but suddenly, skylarks
singing high above the ruins

a black crow
wading in the pond
catching minnows
necessity is
the mother of invention

hands full of weeds
he passes the window
where I sit
there, he says, *all done*
I weep and don't know why

even dry dust
holds some magic
in a speck
we can find history,
riddles, and gold

over lunch
we talk of religion
and world travels
and the mating habits
of the great leopard slug

he puts me
in his inside pocket
close to his heart
I sleep there, unborn
waiting for the light

how green
the new willow leaves
in the sun
how fast the river flows,
how far away you have gone

Irish whiskey
the best dampener
for this pain
four-leaf clover growing
out of a crack in the wall

a buxom wench
in the dated novel
I'm reading
once I might have been
described that way

screaming gulls
follow the ploughman
and his great horse
the field furrowed by day's end
he sleeps like the dead

circling smoke

going indoors,
I say goodnight
to the sky
and the year's first swifts
come screaming over my head

home
is there a word that means
so much?
where we belong
where our roots hold fast

madwomen

uneasy
in the women's presence
I withdraw
my defences the walls,
the windows, the silence

the old aunt
wears thick longjohns
in the heatwave
she wears no bra
not caring about gravity

she said
there's an empty space
in my head
pushing everything away
since my son died

the old aunt
touches her own face
while we talk
she is puzzled by things there
that make no sense

the old aunt
complains of 'wiggly worms'
in her head
she says they wander
behind her eyes, in her brain

circling smoke

the old aunt
makes us read the Bible
in the alleyway
read it aloud, she says,
so I know what to do next

the old aunt
tells her tale to all
who pass by
she is cross with God
who does not grant her wish to die

her frail voice
on the telephone
says goodbye
the old woman of faith
going to meet her maker

my old aunt turns
her face to the wall
ready to die
ninety-seven in March, when
the winds and rains have their way

I tell her
again and again
to lie low
too late, he touches her hair
and she is lost

his lovely girl
with straw-blonde hair
and pale skin
and sweet smiling face
her bitten fingernails, painted black

such scandal
the young teacher, the student,
running away
we all learn how to love
by making mistakes

young thin waitress
only the strong survive
tattooed on her chest
the italic words shielding
her heart's fragility

a widow now
she sells her house
to travel the world
even death in a far country
is better than the void

in Siberia
they throw her off the train,
permit expired
she rides to Latvia
with a huge Russian trucker

circling smoke

alcohol
taking its toll
on my friend
her undyed roots
white in the black curls

one a.m.
the mad woman next door
is chopping wood
I pray for a night storm
to drive her to her bed

haystacks burn
in the tinder-dry fields,
where is the rain?
the clouds are as mad
as the old lady next door

the woman next door
always drunk and undressed
is taken away
on the ward, no brandy,
no cigarettes, no hope

unearthly
the next door cats howl
at my window
no lights on at her house
wondering, I fall asleep

the clock strikes three
as a woman sits weeping
in the old church
she lights a small votive candle
for her gravely ill friend

empty house
at the end of the lane,
a sad sight
I miss the morning smoke
rising when she lit the fire

at lunch he tells me
his grandmother grew old
in the asylum
the bright café overlooks
its blackened chimneys

in the garden
of her old cottage
the crooked tree
she comes no more
to pick the purple plums

there's a cottage
at the end of the long lane
by the railway tracks
it shakes when the train passes
but someone still lives there

her grey body

in autumn
I dream of the pika
gathering grass
hoarding wildflowers for her bed
ahead of the winter snows

I carry the smell
of herbs upon my hands
the rest of the day
like old women, picking
supper greens from the hedgerows

on the cliff edge
walks an old woman, talking
to herself
through her grey body
I see the waves breaking

on a cliff
above a Welsh cove
an old cottage
a gentle ghost
neatly folds back the quilts

cold grey cave
deep in the chalk cliffs
above the wild sea
even with the fire burning
the chill settles in my bones

circling smoke

in crumbling cliffs
the mud and straw shapes
of ancient huts
flint tools, animal bones
mammoth tusks, old dreams

the old men
gathering samphire
on the shore
leaning on sticks, listening
to the siren-song of the sea

the ghost ship
listing on the deep rocks
her next life
a home to fish and weed
a slow decline, back to the sea

the tsunami wreck
settles now on the seabed
off Alaska
burial at sea, I guess,
is a fitting end for her

rough-shelled limpets
cling to the rocks
on the northside
barnacles on the broken boat
mussels on the seabed

I cannot look
at the old worn oak oar
where it lies
the wind, blustering
calls me to the sea again

a low voice
carried on the wind
on the tides
pulls my sorrow
over the hills and far away

daughters

carrying my newborn
up the worn stone steps
to the shrine
forty years on, the same steps
on the cover of his book

Lily loves smarties
but not the blue ones; she says
'blue is for flowers
and sea and sky and my eyes'
and she feeds me all the blues

midwinter, deep snow,
and the bus stop half a mile
from the little house
where the girl stands waiting,
her torch beam lighting the way

listening
to my daughters' laughter,
I remember
childhood games; I imagine
old women reminiscing

my daughters
sitting by the river
at the old pub
late sun sparkles on the water
shines on one fair head, one russet

circling smoke

my daughters have come
not only from my body
but from some deep, far, distant soul
they shine, like stars,
in the darkest of night skies

walking
deep in conversation
up the hill
my lovely daughter
my man in his black suit

a pair of ducks
on the village pond
a willow tree
a clump of daffodils
her quiet prairie voice

five silver spoons
in a brown paper package
from the wide prairie
her great grandmother's spoon box
has empty spaces in it

my daughter's house
is home to cats and mice
ants and beetles
she welcomes people
and creatures the same warm way

once again
I track her flight
across the distance
while I sleep, and wait,
she journeys five thousand miles

leaves falling
and in the hedge
tattered nests
like birds, the children
have flown after summer

I am one
of the north folk, my sister
of the south
I hold hard grey flint in my hand
pale sand trickles through her fingers

hand in hand
with my grandfather
down the lane
to the village rain-barrels
to watch the dragonflies hatch

my friend's girl
so very beautiful,
weeding my plot
with grandpa's old hoe
how he would love to see that

yellow chrysanthemums

two old friends
with the same first name
died today
and in all the hedges
uncurling Spring leaves

at the wake
the house fills with guests,
the villagers
outnumbering the bowls
of yellow chrysanthemums

two old friends
both grieving new losses,
in the garage
talking about pistons,
exhausts and horsepower

the wake over,
the chrysanthemum petals
have all fallen
on bare stems, thin new roots,
golden blooms will come again

arm in arm
under the old tree
among the graves
four friends watch the coffin
being lowered out of sight

desolate
they kneel on the hill
where the graves are
high above, a skylark
sings the requiem

dirty white
the feathers of birds circling
above the gravestones
I watch the blue sky
until they are out of sight

white daisies
around broken gravestones
on the hill
I light candles
for those forgotten ones

tall grasses
and thick brambles
hide the graves
no one remembers them
so we read their names aloud

the gravestone
lying half-buried
in the grass
lichen, moss and ivy
hide even the name

no headstones
in the ancient woodland
where my friend lies
wild white daisies
mark his green burial mound

curling upwards
morning glory leaves,
one blue bud
tomorrow it will open
while he remains silent

I want to ask
'do you miss your wife
after so long?'
then I see in his room
a candle by her photo

two old men in brown
stand close together, talking
of roses and lawns
and paths and flowerbeds and
now and then, of their dead wives

I am trying
not to think of the years
that come after
such grief is too deep
to bear more than once

walking the labyrinth

the landlady says
that ghosts are haunting her pub
on cold mornings
she finds her softest chairs
have moved closer to the fire

by dark beams
in the ancient pub
we share lunch
where long-dead monks
prayed and brewed ale

even now, drinkers
at the old pub watch their words
it is holy ground
the buried bones in the yard
have the right to rest in peace

an old man
in the beer garden
ignores us
talking to his greyhound
feeding it crisps and ale

in the church's shade,
among the broken gravestones
the crooked old pub
smells of moss, ale and incense
a cassocked priest haunts the place

circling smoke

in the old hall
where the strangers dwelt
a robed rabbi walks
he repeats the sacred words
there is no flesh on his white bones

the matins bell rings
in the old church, long before
the pub landlord wakes
he'll unlock the heavy door
when the young priest comes knocking

by thatched homes
and ancient walls
we walk, wind-blown
even our voices
snatched away like old ghosts

the young priest came by
while I sat at the ruins
and stopped to bless me
his hand on my head, the sun
on my face, ghosts around us

broken window
in a derelict house
miles from nowhere
a kerosene lantern
burning, draws me in

the old pub
off the beaten track
long abandoned
re-opens, the new landlord
an old grizzled ferryman

at the old pub
a man's scruffy dog
shares my chips
pigeons are noisy on the roof
a smell of mown grass

old legends
of my birthplace
all dark
no light-winged things
to lift the dragging weight

old voices
like smoke from a dying fire
hanging in the air
inaudible outside
the song deep within me

sometimes the dream
emerges from the place
where it hides
I see him in the cloisters
long legs walking the labyrinth

those men don't sleep

a back street
in Great Yarmouth
by the sea
a thin hooker screams abuse
at sailors passing her by

my birthplace
the least godly place
in Britain
more pubs, nightclubs, brothels
more churches where no one goes

the tattooist
a sullen bearded
silent man
reads the small poem, sighs,
starts to ink it on my arm

poverty moans
on the street corners
of this town
the people heavily tattoo'd
their thin dogs scrounge for scraps

showing off
their new tattoos the young men
strip off their shirts
black fish, birds and dragons
on hairless six-packs

circling smoke

stopping for ale
a short-skirted long-legged cyclist
and a tattooed drunk
a brown terrier
runs between the tables

at the old pub
the long-legged woman
and the young men
flirting, filling the space
where their worlds overlap

once again my friend
comes to show me a black eye
bruised knuckles
another pub fight . . . and yet
how gently he takes my hand

on remand
he comes to say goodbye
once again
the tidal pattern
of this friendship

father and son
banned from meeting
by the courts
sit in the tent of the willows
arm in arm, weeping

in the sun
outside the general store
two old men
smoking cigars moaning
about the village youths

solitary
in his prison cell
he writes to me
I am trapped; and he knows,
paralysed, I understand

in his cell
he dreams of freedom,
his spirit
gone to ground amid
the long grass in the field

when he writes,
his favourite words
are dark
'bleak' and 'grim' and 'gloomy'
and yet how much light he holds

in prison
he makes fast friends
with the governor
working on an early release
for his return to re-offending

circling smoke

it is said
that the city never sleeps
day or night
but dazed and dumb it stumbles
through the long centuries

some lifers live
in the grim hanging cells
where rats run
and the floors hide old bones
those men don't sleep, they go mad

winter full moon
and another young man
in his grim cell
hangs from the bars where dim light
struggles through the dirt

his cellmate hanged,
his daughter in hospital
with an overdose
the governor puts my friend
on suicide watch

in prison, he says
everything he loves
has been lost
all he has left is more time
and bitter regrets

imprisoned
until springtime comes,
he sends a friend
to watch over me
until he is free again

a brown-eyed child
in her feathered hat
waits in the lane
her father will not return
until she is a woman

graffiti
on the boarded-up house
on the corner
Sammi-Lou, I miss you,
please come home

on the windy hill,
fallen stones and ruins
in the fields
beside the rusting iron cages
where the lunatics lived

the long-tailed magpies
in all their cruel beauty
are gathering now,
bickering, fighting, mating
'one for sorrow, two for joy'

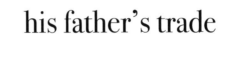
his father's trade

such blue eyes,
this American child
who takes my hand
pulling me close, saying
I want to tell you a secret

talking at the gate
to the leaf-sweeping boy
who grows so tall
every word he says
is carefully considered

I watch the boy
arranging garden stones
in a spiral
his focus on each stone
and its place in the circle

the choosing of stones
seems such a small thing
and yet he is
making order of his life
within the circling stones

the boy
is of two parts: playing
then thinking
he says all things
like coins, have two sides

the hermit crab
lets it all pass by
its curled shell
the boy's still centre
never disturbed

a new friend
this shaven-headed boy
sweeping leaves
who prays for wisdom
and says Life is God is Life

he does not know
a weed from a rose
this rough lad
and yet he tells me
about telekinesis

'smell' he says
holding a crumbled leaf
to my face
at once, I am his age
behind the school shed

young man
who skipped years of school
reads my tanka
in silence, then says
he is going to write a book

the boy comes
covered in cement
from mending walls
he says he is a slave
learning his father's trade

he listens,
silent while I speak
watching me
then he says a few words:
trust, truth, life, death, reasons

I ask the boy,
how are you so wise
so young?
he says, *disappointments*,
and shrugs, and smiles

in the brown eyes
so like his father's
there is peace
this boy has grown wise,
he has found himself

though the boys
swept the paths clean
yesterday
red hawthorn berries
cover the worn steps

his father
on the run from the law
he plays hide and seek
with his little brother
among the greenhouse plants

in the great court
before the bewigged judge
the boy stands
he swears to tell the truth
he lies, saving his father from jail

the boy
clearing my paths
of new snow
his father calls from prison
to say *I love you son*

the boy wants
to put a gun under my bed
just in case
I am under attack
and he does not hear me calling

the young man
walks in his overgrown field
through tall grasses
the field edge is out of sight
the sky above is blue

deformed hens
he gives them a safe home
and talks to them
he says, in time
they will understand

the Egyptian geese
have built a nest in the thatch
the roof lets in rain
he should evict the geese,
but he waits till the goslings fly

he blows into bowls
his breath into boxes, bags
and boots, blowing out
the dry dust and dirt, breathing
his clear spirit into things

the boy works
uprooting bindweed
disentangling
freeing the held roses,
singing, smoking a roll-up

he stands
his hand in the hand
of his grown son
this hard man, this offender,
this protector, this friend

mothers

she kneels
among the lavender
at the gate
for a moment, time stops
then a door slams, a car starts

my old mother
needing new shoes,
buys two pairs
wears blue on the right foot,
red on the left

day is done
old people go to their beds
at the Home
she waits in her Sunday best
for a ride to church

my mother sings
old familiar hymns
all day long
even her spoken words
are small sacred songs

a mad day
at the old folks' home
singalong
my mother the only one
singing the right song

circling smoke

her voice
weak and wavering
sang to me
my birthday is happy
because of it

in the nursing home
she sits singing low
her soft lullaby
my old mother stirs
and listens, entranced

in the old folks' home
the sunday service ends
one lady stays
sitting in her chair
dead before the last hymn

my old mother
once busy knitting
sewing, painting,
now dozes, and watches
rain running down the window

my mother
sleeping all day
in the chair
all night in her bed, ready
for the last long sleep

my mother
grows closer to her end,
that's OK
she knows where she is going
just let it be gently kind

muffled
the sound of the train
passing by
may her own passing
be as quiet and as quick

at the door,
I'm waiting for the child,
and wondering
does he sense the dying
of his great-grandmother?

in the end
we may not have time
to say goodbye
how will I live
knowing she left alone?

his mother gone
the funeral over
the guests leaving
he polishes every inch
of the old motorbike

circling smoke

at the home
where his mother died
he watches
a young African girl
mopping floors

heartbroken
at his mother's death
and sleepless,
he goes out in the cold wind
to feed the small birds

every day
the thin old man
walks the lane
and comes to my door to say
I miss her so much

two for joy

two magpies
on the broken chimney
in the sunshine
sometimes, despair is deep
but it's 'two for joy'

bare trees
beginning to show
signs of Spring
deep within myself
new cells are stirring

I want a lilac
a small tree in a big pot
which will do nothing
but sit with green leaves until
a brief, sudden, purple glory

finally
enough sun to charge
the solar cells
our outdoor Christmas lights
shining bright, in March

the green glass ball
hanging in the window
catches the sun
a small turning on a string
the earth spinning in space

circling smoke

so thin and fine
the silver needles
in the clear quartz
so the slivers of hope
still shining bright

stunted tree
since the harsh pruning
wild with blossom
who could believe you would
so repay my cruelty?

suddenly
birds begin to gather
in the young tree
it has grown enough to shelter
the small winged things

distracted
by shadows of clouds
crossing the field
I stumble upon
a patch of bluebells

under the hedge
a small green bottle
soiled and stained
I breathe the old scent
of april violets

washing earth
from the green beans
I slip away
wanting to be that small mouse
raiding the vegetable patch

pale blossom
on the dark green privet
the scent
goes to my head
like whisky, like love

wanting a garden
filled with scented violets
on a whim
I buy the old
devon violets perfume

such a clattering
the cleaning lady is here
scrubbing and singing
my floor shines like the sun
my dishes sparkle like stars

the warblers
back from Africa
are singing
I envy their small songs
their wild long journeys

circling smoke

he comes now
the good samaritan
over the hill
lifting me into the rough cart
he leads the old horse along

I just want
to sit in some quiet place
and write poems
but oh, the lovely world
keeps knocking at my door

the spiders have awoken

tiny footprints
and a brush of tail
on white snow
tracks to where the seed lies
and back to the hole in the fence

no bats now
flitting over the roof
catching flies
my dreams are sparse now
waiting for spring

in the night
a meteorite shower
and a light frost
this morning, white butterflies
in the sun, and my friend, smiling

in the night
another small spider
finds its way
along the sheets,
tiny feet across my face

on the white wall
a big grey moth
with folded wings
my mind is never still
thoughts fly back and forth

circling smoke

not yet March
and already the spiders
have woken
thin silk threads blowing
from the bare branches

tiny spider
walking in the shadow
of the old wall
I too stay out of the glare
of the bright spotlights

last week the swifts,
yesterday the cuckoo
today, dragonflies
the signs of summer are here
my heart still covered in snow

tiny spider
walking up my arm,
I lift the thread
it swings to the floor
climbs right back up to my hand

small green spider
on the steering wheel
my driver sighs
it takes me a while to find
the right tree to re-home it

on dark chestnut leaves
cabbage-white butterflies
wings catching the sun
my fragile, flitting dreams
bright against the sadness

a bumblebee
walked across the boy's chest
he stood still
making it welcome
a brief small bonding

doubting God
as Thomas did
so long ago
and yet, the field mice
the beetles, the sky

my cold hand
rests on the warm wood
of the table
if I make a move
the small spider will run

lotus flowers
on the still pond
under willows
I cannot skate on the surface
like the water-boatman

circling smoke

the orange fish
so tiny, is dying
floating sideways
I want to help, but nature
has its own ways and times

a fat spider
sitting at the web centre
like a brown-robed monk
my thin silk catching
poems, visions, love

caught in a web
a thin blue feather
held fast
the spider gone
supper for that small bird

he calls me
from the quiet woods
to tell me
he's watching a nuthatch
hunting beetles in the bark

always busy
his old mind working on things
that must be done
while I watch beetles
wondering what they think

from time to time
my life is hanging
by a thread
I watch the spider swinging
from her strong silk in the wind

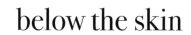

below the skin

the work of healing
goes on deep under
the surface
below the skin,
the flesh, the bones

I long to swim
to feel the weightlessness
of lake water,
heavy as I am
with the burden of pain

gathering
all my lost dreams
together
they don't even cover
the bottom of the pit

in the mirror
not my own face
but another
slowly changing
overlaid with darkness

everything moves
except the pain
I ask the gulls
to carry it to the sea
the wind to take it away

circling smoke

today the pain
eats at my bones
like the mice
the brown harvest mice
in the oat sacks

my fingers
explore the ridges
of many scars
mapping the valleys
where blood rivers ran

I touch
my own broken-ness
like a mother
rocking a child to sleep
like the gentleness of a lover

a treatment
with the consultant
on May first
today is Beltane, he says,
putting on surgical gloves

the learned doctors
testing my paralysis
with a tuning fork
say that it has grown deeper
I hear my body singing

those long months
in a hospital bed
in a square room
now, roaming out of doors
seems like a miracle

I was shaking
in my bed last night
but not with cold
I felt the helplessness
of growing old

white gulls
are circling on the wind
above the trees
I want wings and flight
instead of stillness and pain

relentless
unremitting pain
came for Christmas
carrying, dark-wrapped,
a gift of light

I long to be
a vagabond, a hobo,
free to wander
anywhere, far away
from this brittle cage of bones

circling smoke

my skin
glows blue and silver
the dark room fills
with the sound of wings and waves
the flying fish are calling

all that I like is brown

on the silver birch
one brown leaf on the top branch
the rest have fallen
hold on, small brown leaf, trembling
in the falling snow, hold on

tall thin man
eating beef stew and dumplings
at the village pub
a brown butterfly settles
on the nettles in the lane

long catkins
fall from the chestnut
in the wind
small brown birds pick seeds
from among the stones

I put on
the same brown clothes
every day
it is useless to try
to compete with the flowers

hearing their stories
from the staff who serve
at the small café
they begin to bring themselves
with the cups of coffee

coffee grains
at the bottom of my cup
remind me
of 'the world in a grain of sand
eternity in an hour'

I sit by the fire
wrapped in an orange shawl
counting brown beads
even with hot coffee
my hands are blue with cold

small things
seem to matter more
these strange days
the smell of coffee
the sun through the oak leaves

all that I like
is brown—the sparrows,
the silent soil,
bark and stem, dark chocolate,
peat and rabbits, his eyes

sepia photo
of some brown sheep resting
in an old barn
cracked beams, straw, and hens
pecking in the dirt—that's all

thoughts of creatures
the deer, the crane, the hare,
bring me comfort
all things must suffer
man and bird and beast

on the lawn
in my nightgown
after dark
the full moon rises
the moles come, sniffing the air

we take the old road
out of the noisy city
to another world
a horse and cart comes by
brown cows wander the meadow

still, stealthy,
I slip through the reeds
like a vole,
my pale ears listening
for the splash of the hunter

how can I
be a white woman
in white skin
when I like brown so much
mice, deer, the plain earth

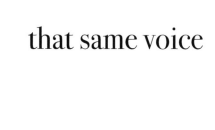
that same voice

on friday nights,
the sound of a hammer
on an anvil
a blacksmith singing
low by the old forge wall

white-haired old man
cleaning my windows
he should retire
he says he is lonely
and what else is there to do?

rooftops
under the streetlight
glittering
a woollen hat
on his white hair

settling to sleep
with thicker blankets
this cold night,
I think of him going out
into his day, into his world

he tells his friends
one by one, using the word
cancer
as if repeating it
will grind it into dust

circling smoke

he begins
to write haiku
and does it
as carefully
as he lays bricks

a cold caller asks
will I help to save
the albatross?
the young man stunned
when I say yes

now I have been
in dreams to your bay
where the great ships sail
I hear that same voice
of the sea, calling

he walks alone
across the desert sands
passing by
a tiny green shoot
uncurling into a fern

since I met him
my happiness grew
my sadness too
he stirs the muddy depths
freeing the buried bones

how hard it is
to give when a friend
wants nothing
I go to him
with empty hands

he writes: come close
then, go away
this old man
wanting to be alone
wanting to be loved

he writes,
I was crazy
to let you go
I reply, *letting go is easy,*
it's holding on that's hard

the postman brings
two books from a distant friend
I begin to read
and forget the pain
and the things I have lost

the old man
forgets so much,
asks again and again
when will my wife be home?
I say, *bye and bye*

circling smoke

gulls facing north
in the pouring rain
by the river
stove-smoke rising
from all the squatters' boats

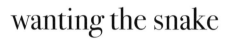

wanting the snake

fieldfares
strip the holly bush
of its berries
my youth and beauty
are a distant memory

I often drop things
and see them laying, but I can't
pick them up again
there are scraps of paper and
small coins all over the floors

my fingers
stroking the new tattoo
on my old stump
wanting the snake to wake
uncoil and fill the space

my tattoos
all swimming, slithering
flying things
as if I knew
walking would be lost

through black kanji
a school of silver fish
one by one
swimming snake-like
across my pale skin

circling smoke

a small pebble
from the river's edge
in my hand
my skin smooth as stone
the stone smooth as my skin

the wind
at the tail of the small train
speeds it along
blows the leaves from the line
snatches the smoke from the stack

back home again
I touch the old walls
fingers on flint
sometimes stone is safer
than fingers on skin

still not ready
for these grinding bones
to be grey ash
I find an old hand
to pull me from the fire

pain in my bones,
I hear them grinding
in the night
can I bear them to burn
or shall I lay them in the ground?

cremation
I decide
not burial
my tattoos going
up in smoke

my friend says:
'when you are about to die
send for me'
can we plan such things?
I say, *let fate decide*

great crane
at the land's end,
is it time?
there are no answers
to any of my questions

over the hills and far away

on the hill
among the twisted pines
the white horse
stands on the stony soil
where Boudicca's bones lie buried

the silver birch
whipped by the wind
dances
thin dark boughs
against the pink sky

in the ruins
ivy covers the bell
the wind
sets it to ringing
songs carry across the fields

two small figures
in the wind-farm shadows,
dwarfed by the sea,
by the great blades turning
through the wide Anglian skies

passing fields
I long to walk there
creep there
between the green blades of grass
over the dark pebbled earth

circling smoke

in a field
black-robed musicians
play Greensleeves
a flock of shaggy sheep
come over the hill to listen

three young men
in the open field
picnicking
sweet smoke and laughter
carry on the wind

music
is filling my head
violins, drums,
wheatfields and the wind
and rain falling on stones

he sings
songs about fields
in autumn
his voice more like
gravel and dust

his one-man path
trodden through the tall grass
winds like a snake
slithering
over the hills and far away

the small footpath
runs across the marshes
to the windmill
bleak without sails
inhabited by sheep

by the ford
in the cow pasture
a young man
playing guitar, singing
songs to the gentle cows

I wept
I want my youth back
and he sang me
a song of rivers,
of loss, and passing time

the black poet
speaking of his England
reminds me
we all came at first
to this land from elsewhere

he slipped through
that long jagged crack
in the floor
and now the music plays
for the quiet finale

circling smoke

he will show up
in some small corner
of my heaven
a wild dandelion
in a narrow field of grass

ringing
in both of my ears
all day long
at night I dream
of sheep bells on the hills

on the air
the heady sweet smell
of wild orchids,
the sound of water trickling
a ditch hidden in undergrowth

Boudicca's Way
leads across the land
to the sea
where once I gathered stones
and shells and salty samphire

beautiful
and ruthless time
nothing
is ever really ours
even our breath, we borrow

every day
more white roses open
on the rambler
every day more
white petals on the path

in the bracken
a long-eared mouse
bird feathers
thin white bones
a copper penny

a black and white cow
ambles across the meadow
to the old gate
I tell her she is beautiful,
her wet mouth green with grass

if I had stayed
in that other land
far away
what would I be doing now?
and who would be walking with me?

the poet says
home is not a place
but a journey
a long travelling
to where we have always been

boy sacrifices

witches, demons
and all those dark ancient spirits
stalk the streets
in the guise of passersby
in the faces of citizens

in the day
the witches work in shops
and city banks
like the owls and their cats
they only hunt at night

solstice night
I asked the witches
about age and death
they smiled sadly at me
and went on dancing

in a night dream
we danced on the winter lawn
to a distant flute
next day I saw wide circles
in the snow, wet shoes by the door

the king's men
turned to pitted stone
by old witches
I long to dance again
in that small grey circle

worn stone steps
down to the ducking stool
on the old bridge
the river passing below holds
no memory of women, drowning

the first frost
and still the fat slugs come
out at night
this cold city top of the list
for child deprivation

the witches
in a dark circle
humming low
no boy sacrifices these days
but still the air heavy with death

the man charged,
the child still missing
presumed dead
how is her mother to bear the grief
when I read the news, weeping?

January
four rosebuds opening
in warm winds
deep snow in the land
where the girl's body lies

the old woman
took the sharpest thorns
from the tree
to sew the burial sheets
the seams speckled with her blood

smooth as silk
tumbled jasper
in my hand
dark red as blood
heavy as old sins

in the cold and dark
bringing the daily news
comes the paperboy
all the world's sorrows
come knocking at my door

night duty
in the old convent
I check the cells
where nuns end their days
and bats squeak down the halls

you would think
after seeing hundreds
that death would bore
each one is as bleak to me
and bright as the ones before

circling smoke

those bodies
I washed and dressed
in white cotton
now lie in rows in my mind
I begin to speak their names

how sad the face
of the thin pale young man
pushing the pram
I can't speak as I pass
the pram is empty

for the dead kids
I light all the candles I have,
say prayers, burn incense
nothing helps the despair,
the horror of it all

in moonlight
a quick dark shadow
outside the window
gone before I know
its name, its purpose

one night at the door
a scratching of fingernails
but no voice calling
only a thick black cloak
lying on the snowy step

a dark morning
black clouds, strong winds
rain lashing
deep underground
my father's bones hear nothing

I rang the bells
again and again tonight
for my friend
they will not disturb his sleep
deep and long underground

the black wand

in little
scrapwood boxes
around the room
Cook's kitchen matches
latte candles, and spells

in the oak cupboard
boxes of beeswax candles
and wooden matches
when I open the drawer
it smells like an old chapel

the woodsman
carving a tiny wand
for the boy
imagine an old man
still believing in magic

how can I
explain to the boy
about magic
while he holds the dark wand
in his small pale hand?

snow and ice
blocked the narrow path
to my holy room
I return in the thaw
to hold the wand's dark wood

circling smoke

the small coins
you call minimal gifts
bring light and luck
copper talismans
of good karma in my hands

seven candles
in my room, seven loves
on my mind,
seven bells on their hooks
the full moon above the roof

candles lit
the first rituals done
and now
the black wand, the sunset mala
begin their dark work

the mala string
back on its iron hook
by the fire
swings gently, still sending
my last silent prayers

how I pretend
that spells and candles
and prayers
can banish sorrows
we must believe in something

in my hand, the wand
small and kindly, holds the black
of the walnut tree,
and its peaceful darkness waits
to shape the spells and sing them

so subtle
the curves where my hand
fits the wand
so gentle the shaping
of the woodman's knife

what is it
about the black walnut
that brings solace?
it's knowing where it fell
the mountains, the wilderness

sacred things
seem to come in threes, they fall
and rise again
I will take three days
to answer the questions

I pass the black wand
through the curling incense smoke
and say your name:
peace to your high mountain home
from my old flint-walled city

circling smoke

end of the day
blowing out the candle
I pass the dark wand
through the last thin drift of smoke
and again bless the woodman

just enough space
in the long oak box
for the dark wand
and for my sadness for him
to fill the gaps

sometimes
a box holds
something puzzling
even empty
it holds blessings

why do I
ring the little bell
when I leave?
the sea-watch always ends
when the eighth bell rings

dear friend

we search
for even the shadow
of a God
and by the roadside,
a ragged man, begging

my soul yearns
and does not know for what
or for who
only that religion falls
where faith stands watching

in my mind
Moses stands always beside
the burning bush
does God only speak to us
in fire and flame and heat?

I lit candles
in the ruined church
and I wept
where is the God
to save me from myself?

sanctuary,
such a shining word,
like shrine, sacred, silence
but how barren
rites, religions, rules

circling smoke

sunshine
on the old stone walls
of the church
the organ playing
makes me wish I believed

he struggles
with the first seven books
of the Bible
when he gets to meet Ruth
then his joy will return

I would be
a sweeper of church floors
working slow
in shadows and silence,
alone with gods and ghosts

more flint falls
from the crumbling walls
of the old church
among the worn gravestones
bright clumps of bluebells

the travertine
is cold to the first touch
and heavy
the corn goddess
grows warm in my hand

corn tithe mark
in the flint pebbles
of the ruin
this ancient church was paid for
by the sweat and toil of peasants

the sound of hymns
echoes from the knapped-flint church
high on the mound
the bones of bronze-age chieftains
lie silent far below

overgrown
between the stones
rough grasses
once worshippers gathered
now just thistledown

needing
no father
at my age
I begin prayers
with *dear friend*

Turin shroud
carrying the image
of such a dear face
does it matter
what his name was?

circling smoke

the old man
holds onto rituals
in lieu of hope
the meaning of his life
safe in five-line poems

round towers
on the little flint churches
in old Norfolk
no square edges, no corners
where the dark devil can hide

in the ruins,
cigarette ends,
an empty bottle,
and on a broken wall,
graffiti—*religion sucks*

periwinkle
a thin purple-flowered snake
creeping over rocks
searching for the crevices
and cracks in my soul

my spirit
a tissue-paper kite
lifting, falling
please don't let go
that long string

this year for Lent
we will give up worrying
and fretting, and trust
that life will be forgiving
when we are frail and careless

scaffolding
on the crumbling tower
of the Viking ruin
once, thick stems of ivy
held it safe and steady

the little bronze monk
sat once more today
in the hands of the gypsy
how good it must be to feel again
the kind rough hands of the maker

coiling

drawing snakes
curling around things,
serpentine
even the word is coiled,
sleeping in my head

my well-being
swings on a fragile thread
caught by the wind
I'm tossing the coin
for holding on, letting go

my skin peels
from my fingertips
in summer
the snake in the grass
looks at me with grey eyes

all night
small noises on the stairs
up and down
and up again—the old cat
restless to go hunting mice

I scattered mealworms
the blackbird came back
yellow-beaked, thin
the female just bones now
buried under the hawthorn

pondering
distant planets
and black holes
the little train steams by
on its way to the coast

I have no servant,
I ring the maid's bell myself
when supper is made
I love the song of the bell
sounding through the quiet house

old worn penny
once it was enough
to buy for a man
a tankard of ale
a night with a woman

midnight
at the end of the tenth year
I breathe again
the milestone passed
the road goes on

spinal bones
loosening, shifting
trap a nerve
its garbled messages
go singing down the wires

in the night
hail lashed the windows
winter returned
I woke coughing
the curtains soaked

aphasia
all those lost words
I could not find
coming back, marching
in five straggly lines

grief
burrowing in
like a mole
blind black velvet
with sharp claws

one slow waltz
without music
along the path
beside the rice fields
would have been enough

the wildness in me
dances figures of eight
in the soil
she will still be dancing
when the sea covers the land

circling smoke

the wind blows
in the stone circle
in my mind
bringing the wild smell
of mountain thyme and heather

woolly mammoth
slowly appearing
from melting ice
the ancient permafrost
begins to die

what would I put
in the open mouth
of the snake?
words, small poems, coiling
in circles to the tail

how strange is time!
I sit writing poems
while around the world
my friends write, and sleep
and wake, and work

dowsing
the closer I get
to old poems
the wider
the pendulum circles

in the circle
on the windy hill
a small box
inside, a tied scroll
with the words *there is no end*

due at Christmas

young girl
watering my dry pots
all summer
so lovely, so sad,
and the child due at Christmas

winter displays
flickering white lights
red ornaments
outside, the sweet scent
of daphne in flower

in the corner
of the Christmas grotto
a straw wizard
one small boy whispers to it
ignoring Santa

down the lane
the girls are singing
arm in arm
coming home from the pub
merry as fish-wives

woken in the dark
by the noisy revellers
stumbling home
on the fence, a barn owl
turns its head to watch them pass

thin woodsmoke
from my neighbour's chimneys
and faint laughter
they gather by the fire
getting drunk on ale

Christmas Eve
outside the pub
he falls drunk
and staggers home
with no money, no gifts

no kerosene
for the stove, the old poet
sits in the cold
singing half-forgotten carols
in Japan on Christmas Eve

deep longing
comes suddenly
this Christmas
for the sound of his voice
the touch of his hand

doing time
and missing his girl
at Christmas
a lifer tattoos 'Amy' and a rose
on my young friend's arm

so far away
she sets her alarm to ring
at two am
waking from a deep sleep
to wish me Merry Christmas

text from jail
from a banned mobile
Happy Christmas
sim cards bearing
love and hope

McDonalds
this Christmas holiday
filled with kids
outside, a treecreeper
picking bugs from bark

Christmas Day
I got dark chocolate,
loving calls,
an afternoon nap,
at last, peace

in the next cell
the gentle black man
his new friend
hung himself, at dawn
on Christmas Day

circling smoke

the surgeon
talking of my options
and choices
also tells me he got
a train set for Christmas

a great heart beating

his is a house
that is gently good
and orderly
a house that tells you
about the man inside

male dunnock
feeding the female
beak to beak
my man in the kitchen
scrambling eggs

late breakfast
on the terrace
in the sun
coffee and his quiet voice
enough for this day

who would want
a man who wields power
makes the rules
when you could have one
who brings breakfast and peace?

the male robin
and the small brown female
picking at seeds
sometimes my man and I
spend a quiet do-nothing day

circling smoke

I watch my man
watching the magpies
hunting small birds
on his face the same grief
and awe as I feel

I watch from bed
as my friend works all day
in my garden
love is sometimes cloaked
in sweat and soil

he limps
along the path
to where I sit
I remember making love
where the wild sheep slept

home from work
he recites the places
he has been
his life a picture map
of Norfolk villages

so many
lovers and friends,
in the end
I find the only one
who is both

a partner
should have the best of us,
the gentleness
how often, tired and cross,
we snap at each other

not knowing
what else to do for me
my man brings food
and he prays to his God
to take away the pain

of all the poems
I have memorised
in a lifetime
the one I recite most often
is you

the dolls-house
he built of Swedish pine
tiny windows,
chairs and beds and floors,
and a bright red door

a house with grace
and quiet simplicity
the kind of place
that speaks your name
when you are passing by

circling smoke

I remember
standing young and slim,
child on hip
the old oak in the photo
now has broken branches

old white hair
curling from the back
of his baseball cap
I just want to rest
my hand there

going through
the same routines
each night
candles blown out, door shut,
his book back on the shelf

I rest my head
on the great warm side
of the Bear
my inner world tells me
rest, and bear the pain

under my ear
the great heart beating
he sleeps
I learn to find the place
where it all comes together

a house with no corners

if only I could
live in an old light-house
far out to sea
a house with no corners
and always the light, shining out

loud fireworks
and thick woodsmoke
on the air
who remembers why
Guy Fawkes started it all?

my fingers yearn
for the flat ivory keys
and the thin black ones
to make music, to drown out
the traffic noise, the dripping rain

the small stream
at the edge of the field
is frozen
why do I watch so long,
waiting for something to move?

wrapped in a shawl
in the middle of the day
I catnap
a new habit these dark days
waiting for the Spring

circling smoke

white snow
blowing on this dark day
in March
another birthday comes and goes
pink blossom on the cherry

turning
the ring on my finger
round and round
the words on the silver
to everything its season

I dropped a few lines
on the stone pathway
night rain fell on them
later I found the paper
with no words upon it

I lost my grip
for a brief moment
the wind snatched the poem
and tossed it
over the hills and far away

old trawlerboat
off-shore, ploughing
through low waves
the grief of being landbound
breaks again and again

I lie down
briefly to ease the pain
and the sun breaks
onto my face, and I know
the flipside of sadness

the shadow
of the chimney like a man
on the roof
the thatcher in the day
the fiddler in the dark night

whatever
the distance between us
or the years
as long as I breathe
you are with me still

in the stadium
the countries parading
their flags flying
wheelchair after wheelchair
rolling on by

waddling
up my wheelchair ramp
a fat pigeon
I miss the feeling
of feet on the ground, walking

circling smoke

in my room
the yellow streetlights
cast long shadows
such comfort in those dim shapes
the walls, the floor, the windows

I don't want
to close my eyes now
and stop reading
but it is dark, and the quilt
is heavy, and sleep will come

Afterword

It has been my pleasure to watch Joy develop her distinctive voice and to publish her tanka in the pages of *Atlas Poetica*. When she told me she had written three thousand tanka, I told her she should publish a book. I knew it would be a challenge because Joy is paraplegic after a motorcycle accident. When she asked to hire me to create the book, I agreed.

Joy sent me over 2200 tanka. I read them all, then sorted through them, finding themes and organising them into chapters. We corresponded about symbols, places, emotions, art, and people. She selected a photograph by her friend, Rachel Burch, depicting a labyrinth carved into rock, and I kept that theme in mind while making my selections.

Each chapter may be read as a sequence. Indeed, some of them, such as the 'old aunt' poems, were composed one after another in sequence. Others were written at random times over a period of three years; for example, 'the black wand' is a recurring trope in her work.

All her tanka are intensely autobiographical, but she has a keen sense of herself not just as an individual, but as a social person connected to friends, daughters, husband, family, neighbours, and community. Her connectedness extends to the past; the ghosts of the dead walk the pages of her book as they walk the streets of Norwich. When we meet the young priest who blesses her, we don't know if he is a corporeal person or is the priest that haunts her usual pub.

For that matter, although she is dependent upon a wheelchair, she manages to get out and about: to visit ruins and fields, to go to the pub, to travel the streets of Norwich. She seems to know everyone. Lonely men, serious boys, and even strangers warm themselves in her welcome. They can be found working in her garden or giving her a lift in a field.

circling smoke

They even message her from prison. Joy is a person who can see the good in everyone—including a man convicted of an unnamed crime that will keep him from his family for a long, long time.

Joy has compassion for all creatures: the spider dangling from its thread, mice, birds, madwomen, felons, old nuns, drunks, ghosts, and the unnamed dead with their broken gravestones. To read Joy's tanka is to walk the unseen world that overlaps the streets and fields of her hometown. The veil that separates us from other people, living or dead, is a gossamer that parts when she waves her magic wand.

M. Kei
3 September 2013

Credits

Some of these poems have appeared in:

Tanka Journal
Atlas Poetica
Blithe Spirit
Lilliput Review
Gusts
Haibun Today
100 Gourds
Simply Haiku
Kokako
Red Lights
Ribbons
Skylark

Made in the USA
San Bernardino, CA
19 November 2013